LEARN SCIENCE WITH MO

MACHINES

Paul Mason

Michael Buxton

Enslow PUBLISHING

Published in 2026 by Enslow Publishing, LLC
2544 Clinton Street
Buffalo, NY 14224

First published in Great Britain in 2024 by Wayland

Editor: John Hort
Design: Collaborate
Illustrations: Michael Buxton
Science consultant: Peter Riley

Manufactured in the United States of America

CPSIA compliance information: Batch #CSENS26: For further information contact Enslow Publishing LLC, New York, New York at 1-800-398-2504.

Please visit our website, www.enslowpublishing.com. For a free color catalog of all our high-quality books, call toll free 1-800-398-2504 or fax 1-877-980-4454.

Cataloging-in-Publication Data
Names: Mason, Paul. | Buxton, Michael, illustrator.
Title: Machines / Paul Mason ; illustrated by Michael Buxton.
Description: Buffalo, NY : Enslow Publishing, 2026. | Series: Learn science with Mo | Includes glossary and index.
Identifiers: ISBN 9781978544758 (pbk.) | ISBN 9781978544765 (library bound) | ISBN 9781978544772 (ebook)
Subjects: LCSH: Machinery--Juvenile literature.
Classification: LCC TJ170.M376 2026 | DDC 621.8--dc23

Contents

The words in **bold** are in the glossary on page 30.

Mo's CLUBHOUSE

Mo's friends have come over. Just like EVERY TIME they come around, Mo's room is a mess!

The clubhouse is going to be a place where Mo, Rory, and their friends can get away from grown-ups and make as much mess as they like. (They are going to need some help from the grown-ups to build it, though.)

There will be three steps to create the perfect clubhouse:

1) Design

2) Getting the building **materials** they will need

3) Building

This project is going to be hard work! To make it easier, Mo and friends will learn to use **simple machines**, such as screws and levers. (Their grown-up helpers will also use a few more-complicated machines.)

The first job will be to find a design that everyone can agree on and which will be possible to build!

Machines and FORCES

We often use the word "machine". Machines are things we use to do work, or to make work easier.

A simple machine is something that affects **force.** Forces are what move objects.

Exactly, Mo. Forces can also change the direction or speed an object is moving.

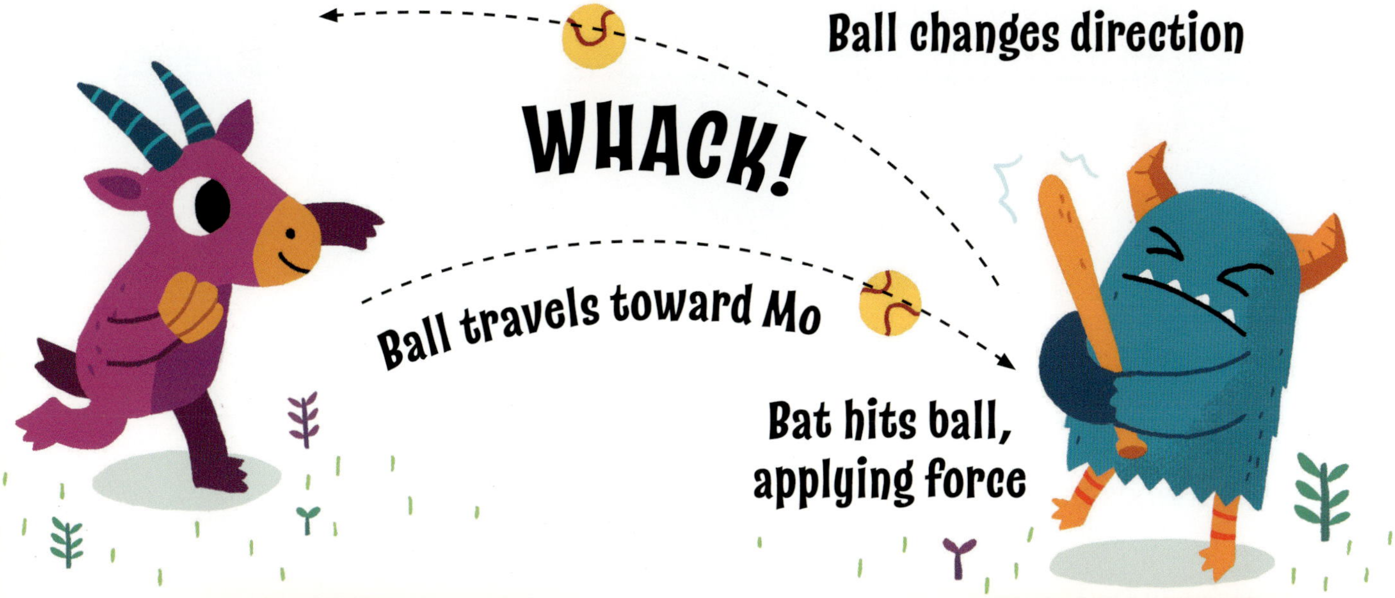

Mo, when you were playing softball, did the ball go a long way?

MILES AND MILES.
IT TOOK LILY AGES TO FIND IT.

Would it have gone as far if you had hit it with your hand, instead of a bat?

NOWHERE NEAR!

The softball bat is a simple machine (called a lever). It changed the direction the ball was moving. It also increased the force of you hitting the ball.

A hammer is the same kind of simple machine: a lever. It makes banging in nails easier.

AS LONG AS YOU DON'T
HIT YOUR HAND!

Clubhouse PLANS

Mo and friends need to think about the design of the clubhouse. At first they all had different ideas about what it would be like ...

BUT NO ONE KNEW HOW TO BUILD A FAIRY CASTLE OR A GIANT TREEHOUSE. SO, IN THE END, AMY DREW SOMETHING WE COULD ACTUALLY BUILD!

Clubhouse plan

Amy's drawing (agreed by the Committee of Friends)

Mo, the next thing is to work out the jobs you will need to do and what tools and materials you will need for them.

1. Materials

Wood for frame

Screws

Brackets (What are brackets? Need to look this up ...)

Wood for roof

Nails

Canvas for walls

2. Jobs

Make sure wood is right length

Screw together frame

Nail down roof

Add canvas walls

Tools

Tape measure

Drill

Screwdriver

Ladder

Hammer

Saw

Good job, Mo, well done! It looks as though you are ready to get started.

Transporting MATERIALS

Mo and the others need to move the wood, canvas and other materials to where it is being built.

The wood was too heavy to pick up.

Dizzy tried pushing it, but it would not slide ...

Even Dizzy and Dozy together could not do it.

Remember we said that machines often make jobs easier? What you and your friends need, Mo, is a machine that can help.

One of the oldest and most useful machines there is: the wheel and axle.

The cart will manage two forces that were making it hard to move the building supplies:

1. Weight

The wood was too heavy for Dizzy and Dozy to carry. Now they have loaded it piece by piece on to the cart, the cart is doing the carrying!

2. Friction

It was impossible to slide the wood along the ground because of a force called friction. Friction is a pulling force between two objects that are touching. The wheels of the cart have much less friction, so they are easier to move.

Now all you have to do is unload everything!

Levering ROCKS

There is one last job before building can start, Mo. You and your friends need to make sure the ground is flat.

Unfortunately, there are two big rocks sticking up right where the clubhouse is going to be!

Oh no!
They might make campouts uncomfortable ...

Don't worry, Sid. To move the rocks, we just need two simple machines. The first is a spade (a kind of simple machine called a wedge). The second is a **crowbar** (a kind of lever). Your mom has come to make sure you use them safely.

THAT MAKES SENSE...

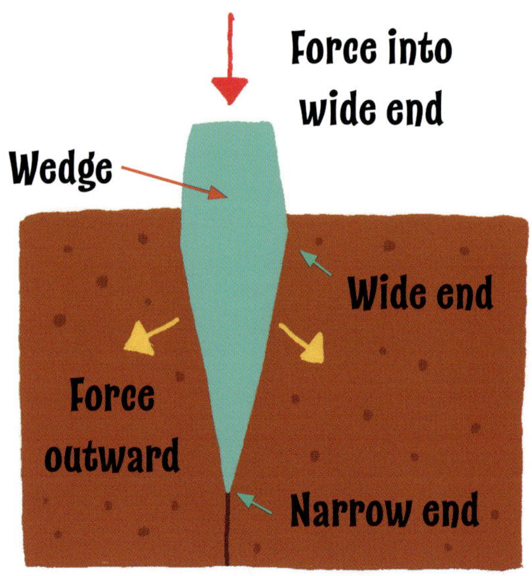

The blade pushes into soil and splits it into pieces, which can be lifted out.

After this, you can move the rock using the crowbar. This is a kind of tool called a lever. Levers change the direction of forces.

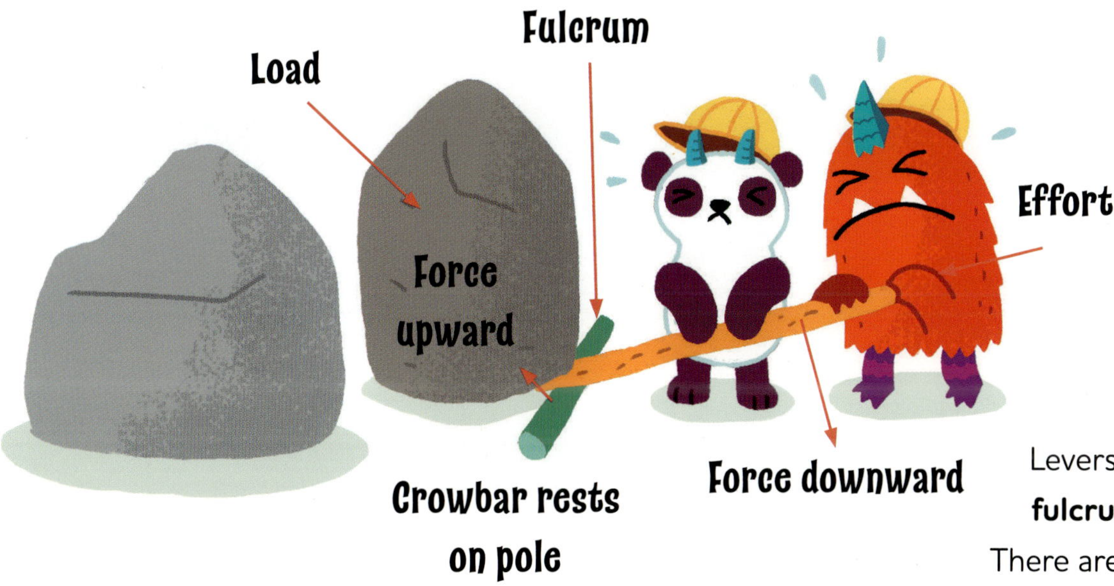

Levers use an **effort** and **fulcrum** to move a **load**. There are three types of lever, which you can read about on pages 22–23.

Mo, can you sort these things into WEDGES and LEVERS?

axe, doorstop, seesaw, oar, nail scissors, wheelbarrow

The answers are on page 32.

Measuring and CUTTING

Now the ground is ready and the materials are all here, Mo, you can start to make the frame of your clubhouse.

First, what wood lengths do you need for the frame?

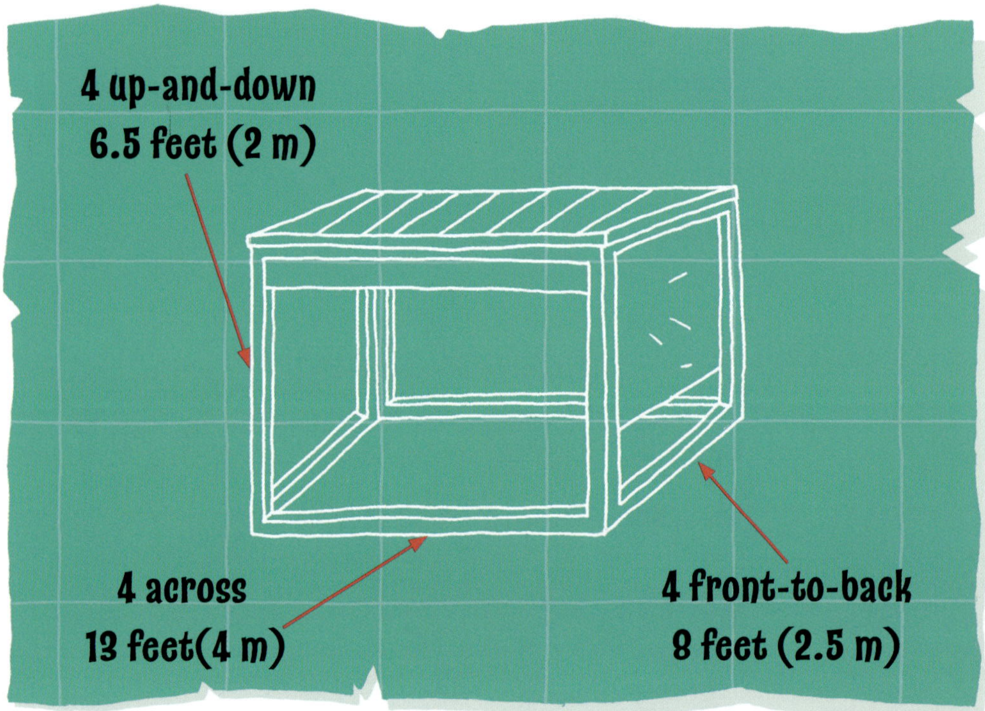

Good job! Now measure your pieces of wood to see how long they are.

Amy's dad has come to cut the wood for you, using a **circular saw.**

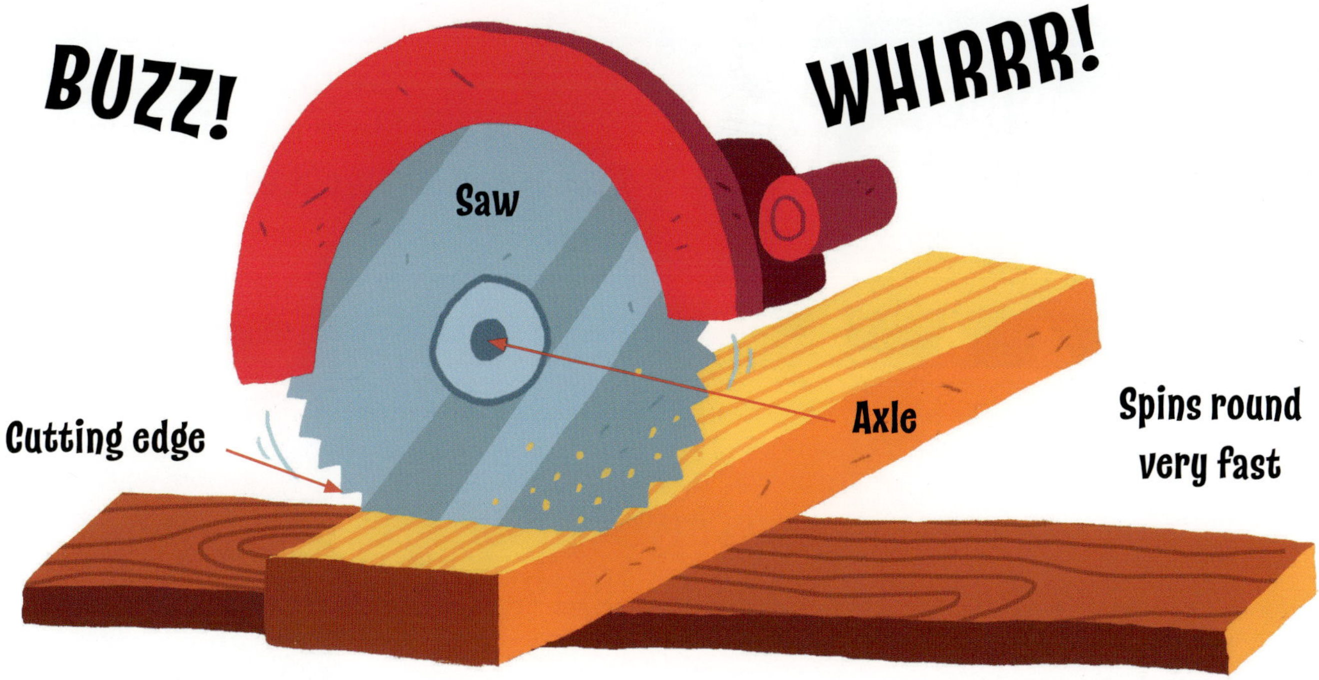

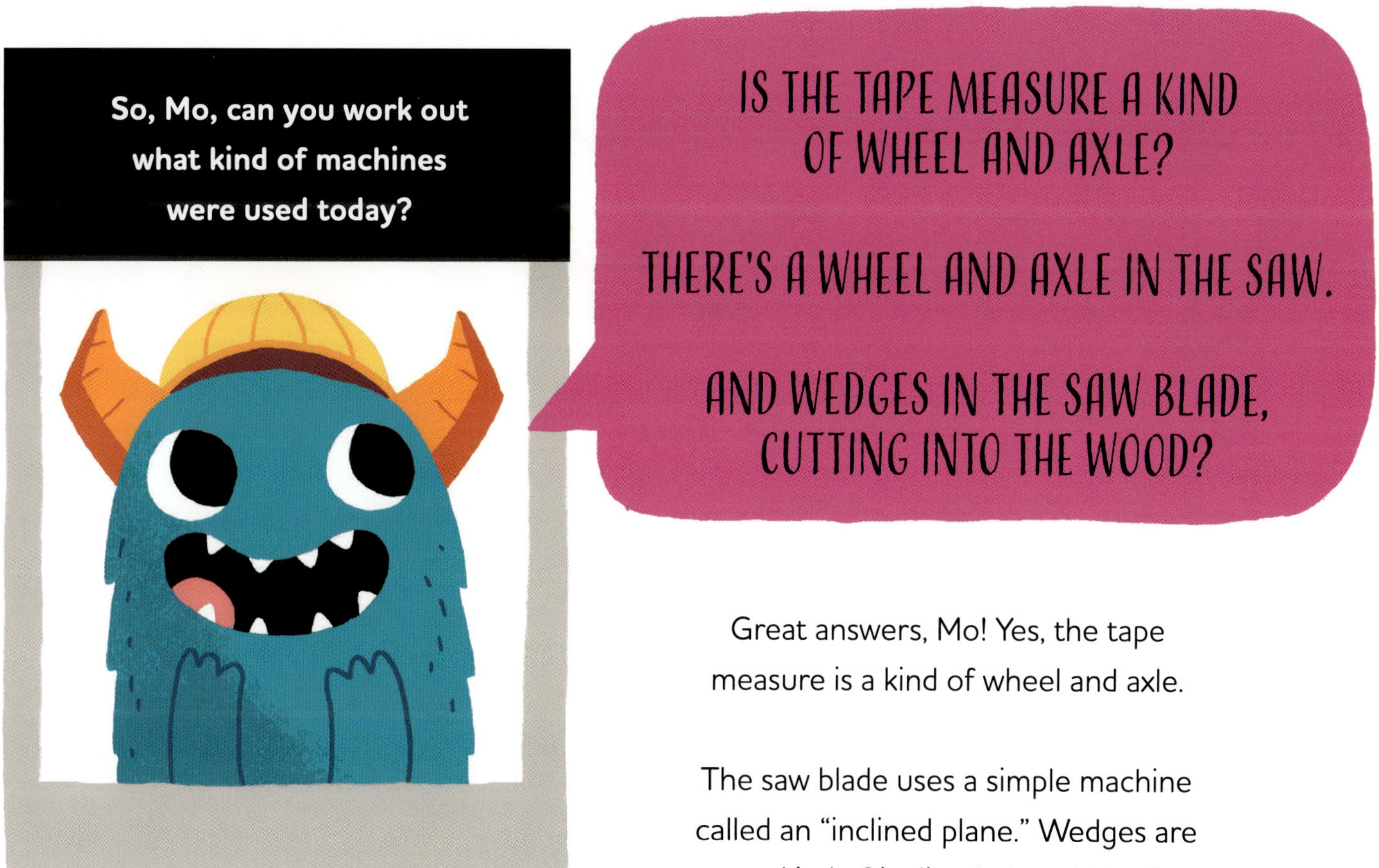

Great answers, Mo! Yes, the tape measure is a kind of wheel and axle.

The saw blade uses a simple machine called an "inclined plane." Wedges are one kind of inclined plane. We will learn more about them on page 24.

Screwing Together THE FRAME

Now the wood has been cut to the right length, Mo, it is time to join the pieces together.

We are going to use a simple machine called a screw. A screw is a cylinder with a **spiral** ridge or groove.

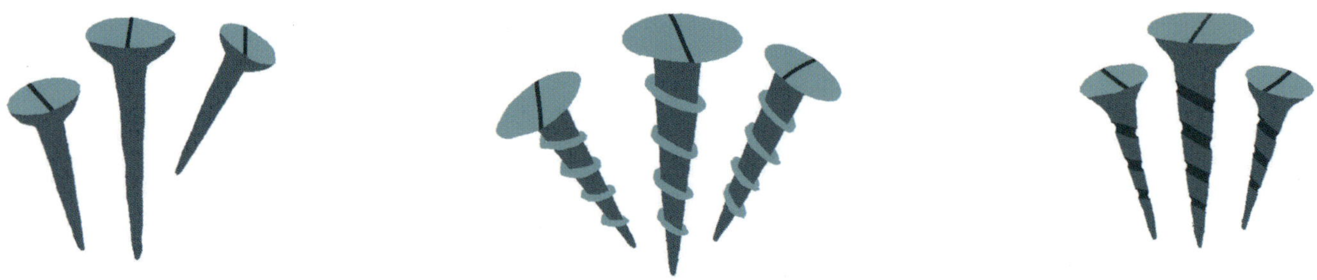

Cylinder **Ridge** **Groove**

Screws change a turning force into a pushing or pulling one. The first screw we are using is a drill.

Sorry, Mo, that's a grown-up's job.

The drill changes a turning force into a pulling force. It pulls out wood and makes a hole.

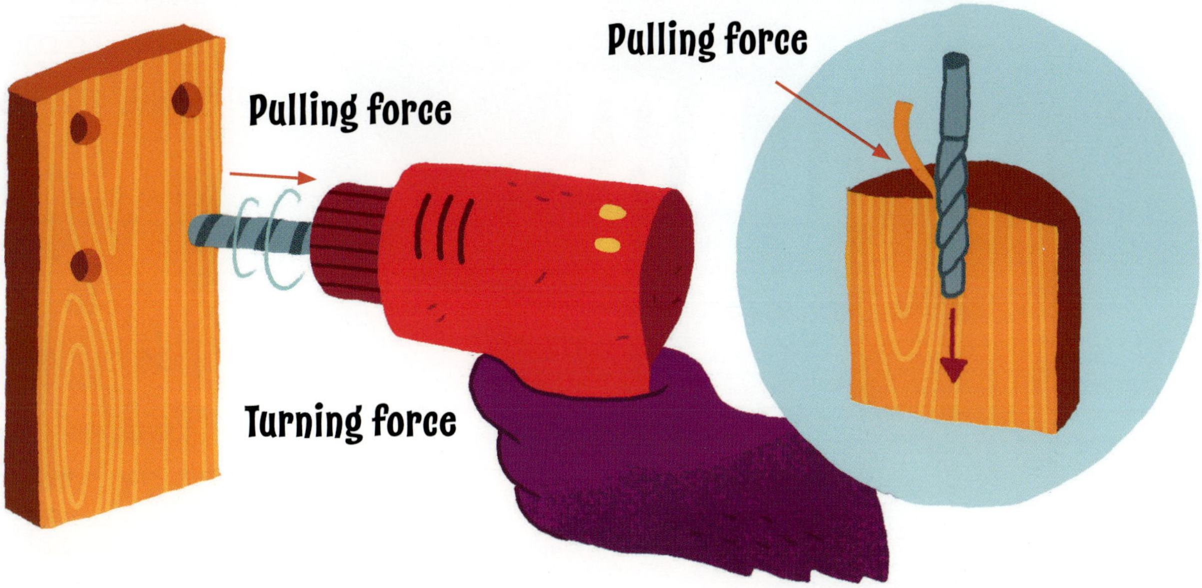

Now it is your turn, Mo. You and Amy are going to use screws to join the pieces of wood together.

Good work, Mo and Amy! Now let's do a quick quiz to see what you have learned about screws:

1) How did the screws change a turning force?

2) What might happen if the turning force was reversed?

Find out if your answers were correct on page 32.

Lily Gets IN GEAR!

The next job is nailing down the clubhouse roof. But no one can find any nails!

No problem. Your ride to the shop and back will be a great chance to find out.

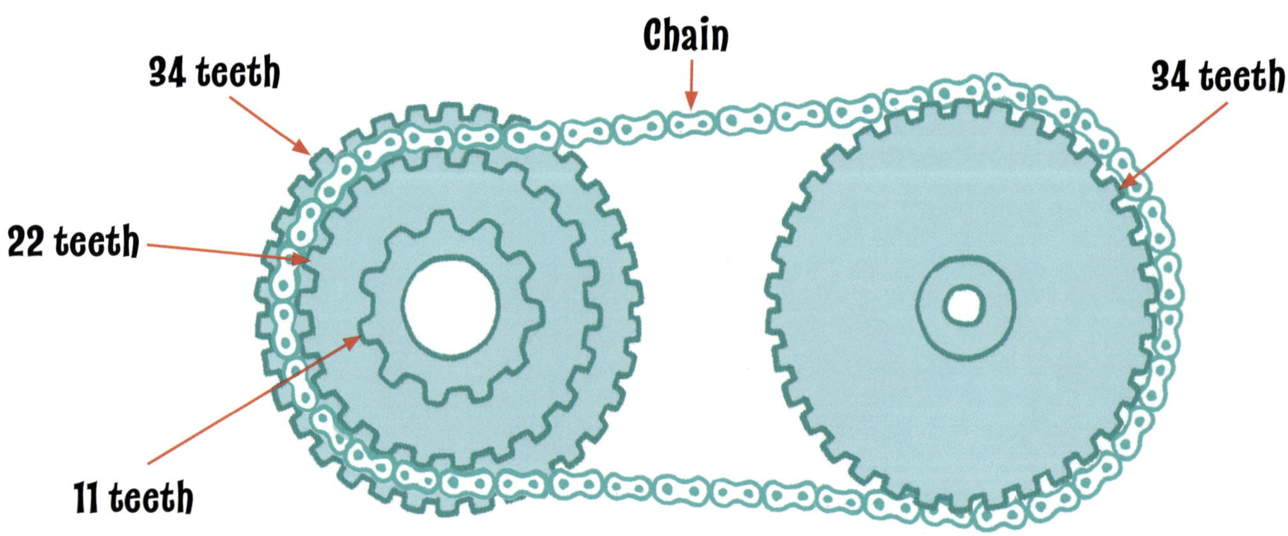

We use gears to affect force. Easier gears spread out effort and harder gears make the effort shorter but more difficult.

On flat ground, Lily whizzes along in her middle gear ...

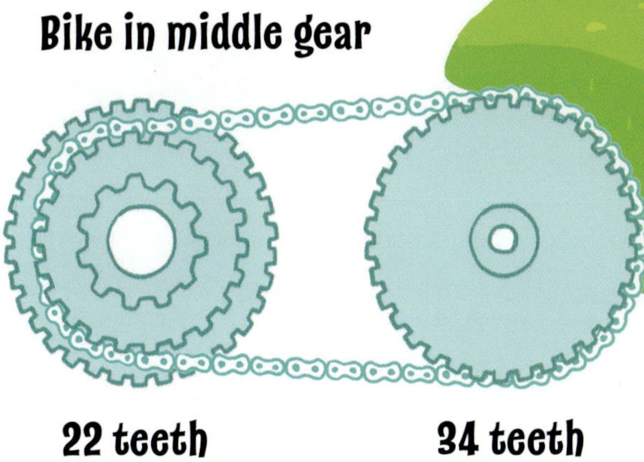

... but then the road starts to go uphill. Lily, you need to change gear! Put the chain on the biggest cog.

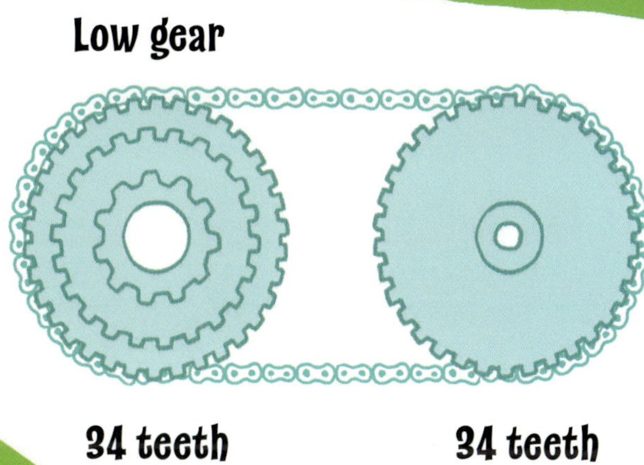

That's right, Lily. Every time you turn the pedals, the back wheel travels a shorter distance than before. The gear has spread out your effort.

So, which cog are you going to need on your way back down the hill?

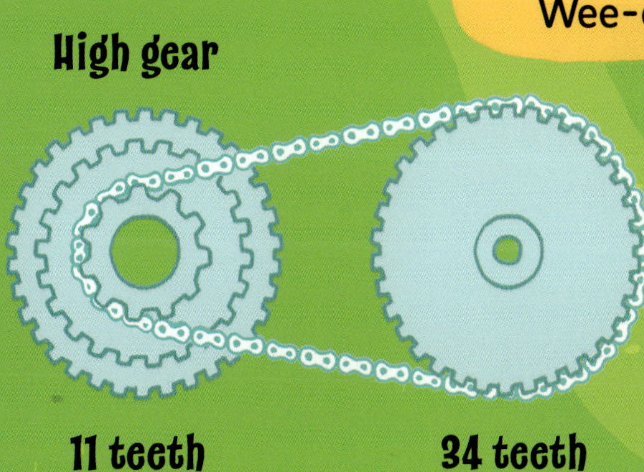

PLANKS AND PULLEYS

Rory is going to build the clubhouse roof.
Rory loves climbing and whizzes up the stepladder.

PLANKS CAN'T CLIMB, THOUGH. HOW CAN WE GET THEM UP THERE?

Mo, we are going to use a machine called a pulley. Pulleys can make a job easier by changing the direction of a pulling force.

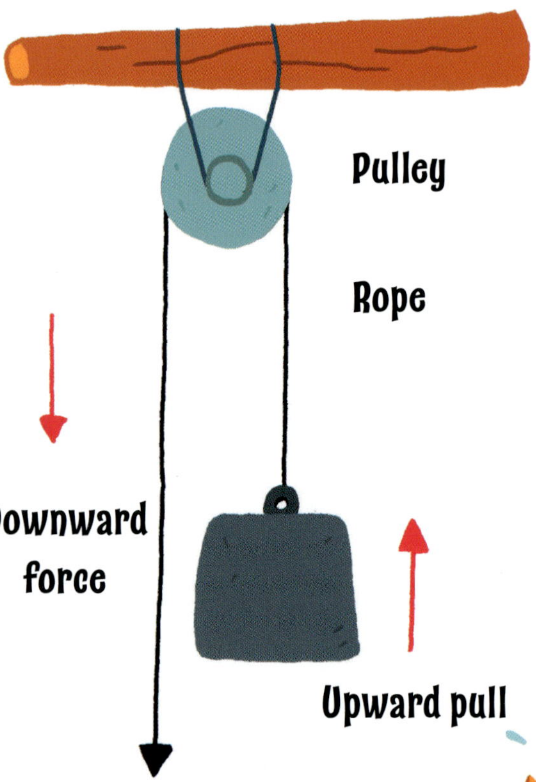

If Rory climbs up a tree and ties a pulley to one of the branches, it will be easier to lift planks up to Rory.

THIS IS STILL HARD WORK, THOUGH ...

Using more than one pulley together makes it even easier to move a load. (The rope will have to be pulled further, though, because simple machines cannot change the total amount of work needed to do a job.) We need more pulleys!

Mo, can we check that you and Rory will remember how pulleys work?

How do pulleys affect force?

Does having more than one pulley make things easier or harder?

Does having more than one pulley mean you have to use less effort or more?

Find out if you were correct on page 32.

Different Kinds of LEVER

Now Rory is going to nail the roof planks in place. Once this is done, it will really start to look like a clubhouse.

Rory is going to use nails to fix the roof planks to the frame.

I LOVE hitting nails with a hammer! Bash! Bash!

Then this is the ideal job for you, Rory. Which two machines will you be using to do it?

Easy: the hammer! No, wait ... TWO machines?

Yes. The hammer is one, you are correct, but a nail is also a machine. It is a kind of wedge.

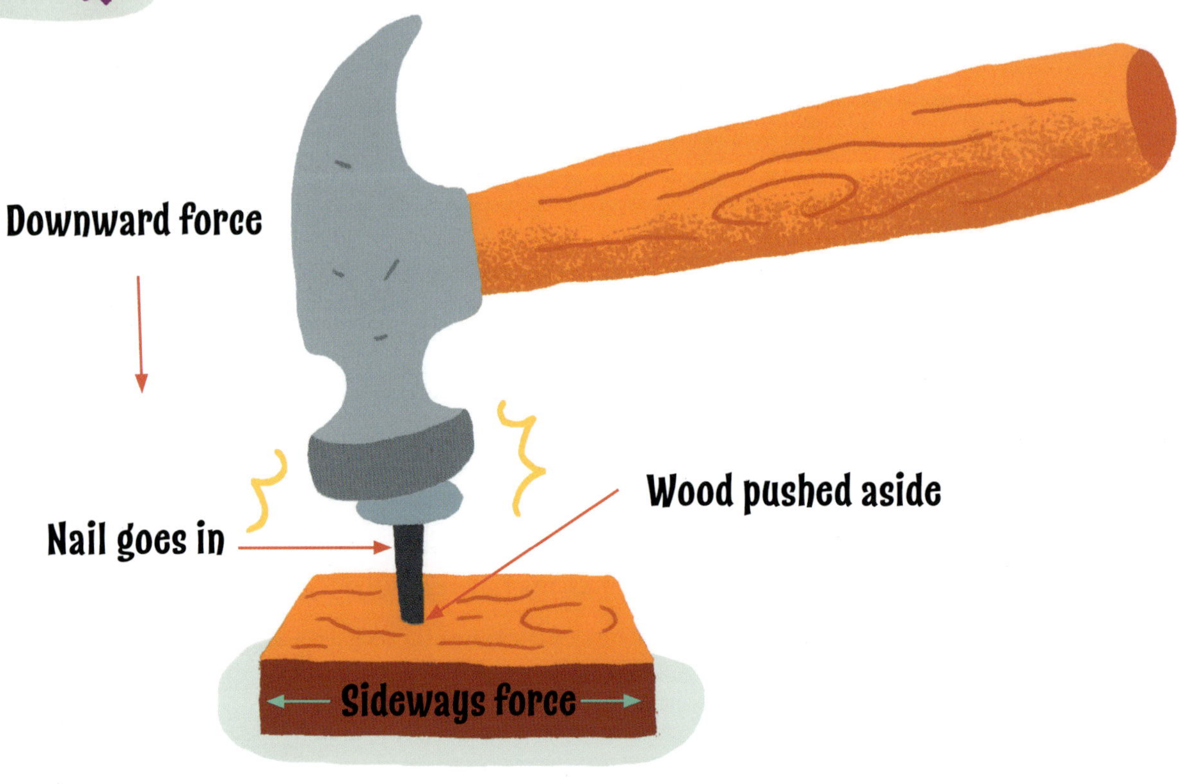

Rory's hammer is a kind, or "class," of lever. There are three of these:

Class 1

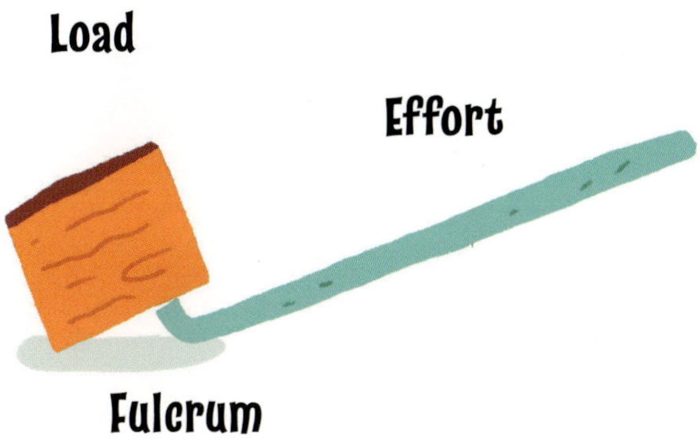

Class 2

Class 3

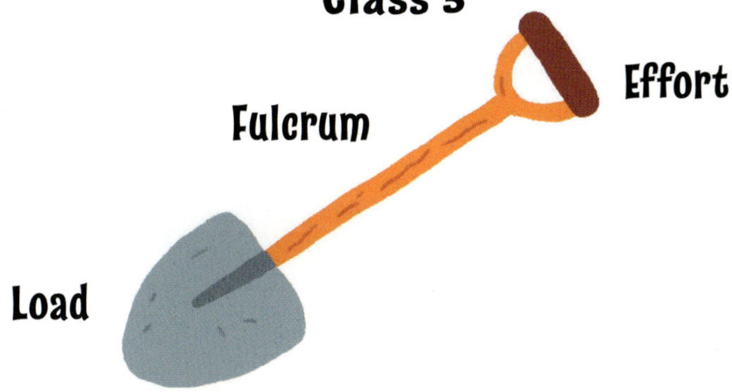

Which kind of lever is your hammer, Rory?

Can you help Rory with the answer while he does the work?

Find out if you were right on page 32.

RESCUING RORY!

Rory is hammering in the last nail on the roof when disaster strikes. The hammer hits Rory's thumb. Ow!

Don't worry, Mo. We can rescue Rory using a machine called an inclined plane.

An inclined plane is a slope. It changes the amount of force needed to move a load. Just like with the pulleys on page 21, though, the load will have to be moved further if the effort is less.

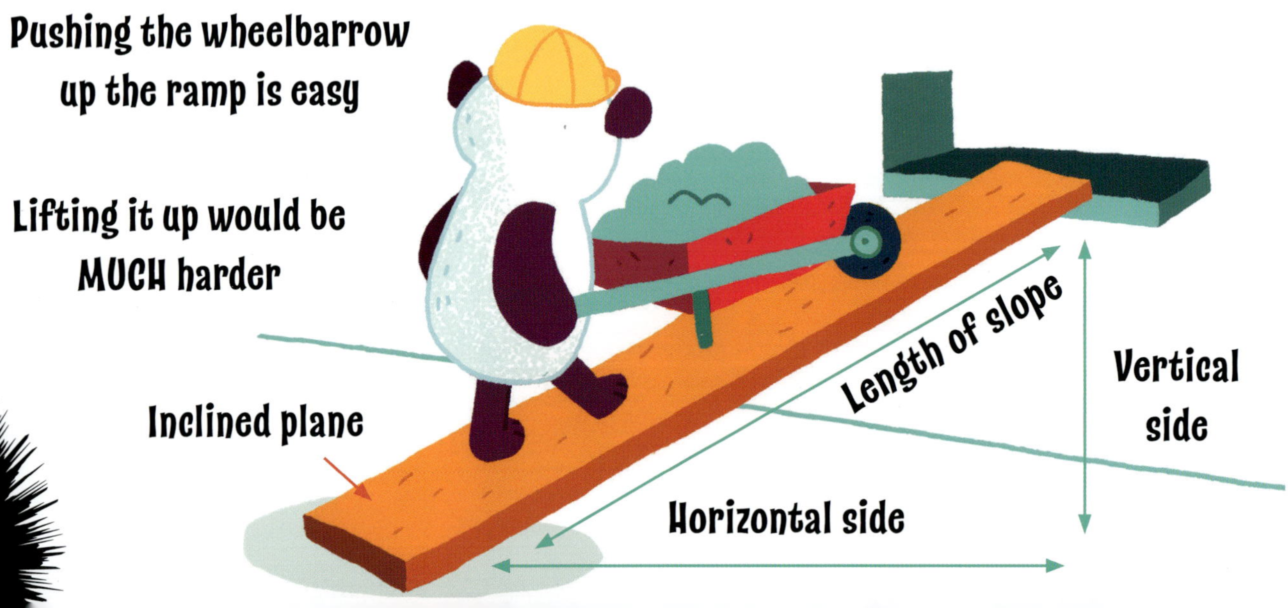

Mo, if you lowered Rory down an inclined plane, do you think it would need more force or less than lowering straight down?

The friends lean up a wide plank ... ... then lower Rory safely down.

Great job, Mo (and friends). While Rory is going to get a bandage, can you think of some other inclined planes we use?

Yes, great answers. Those are all inclined planes.

Walls and WINDOWS

The last job for the clubhouse is to add the canvas walls.

Fortunately, a grown-up has already cut the pieces of canvas to the correct size using scissors. What kind of machine are scissors, Mo?

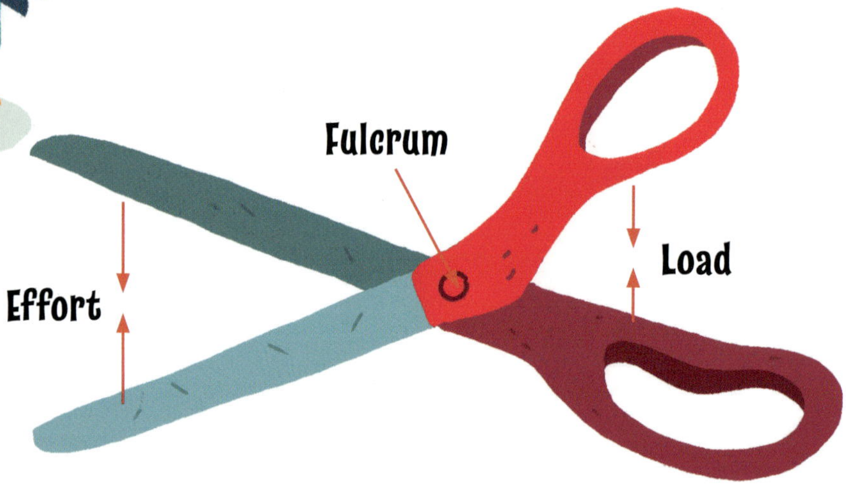

Excellent answer, Mo, correct. Can you think of other tools with more than one lever that we use?

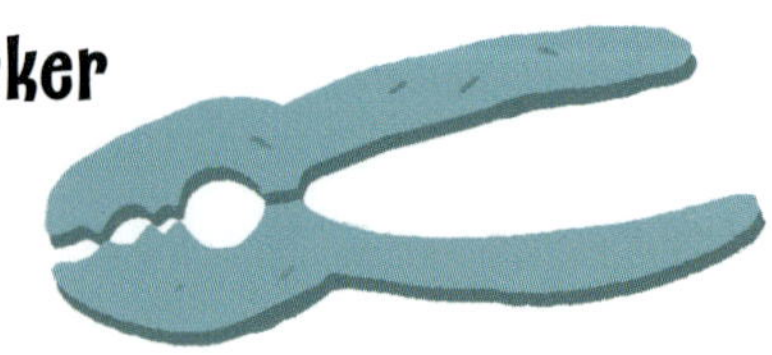

Well done, Lily!

To fix the canvas to the walls, first the friends wrap the ends around wooden battens (long flat strips of wood). They screw the battens to the top of the frame. Now the clubhouse really looks like a clubhouse!

Amy's idea is probably best, Mo. Machines such as pulleys, levers, inclined planes, screws, wheels and axles, and wedges make lots of jobs easier, but not all of them.

Monster MARSHMALLOWS

The clubhouse is finished! Tonight the friends are having a party. Their grown-ups have offered to get a campfire ready.

First, the logs for the campfire arrive on a cart.

Next the logs need to be cut into smaller pieces.

Once the fire is going, the friends decide to toast some marshmallows. Rory cuts open the packet with some scissors.

Everyone pushes their marshmallow on to a stick. At first, Lily's does not go on properly:

One of the grown-ups sharpens Lily's stick:

Now everyone can toast their marshmallows!

Can you list all the machines that Mo and his friends have used on this page?

Glossary

bracket
specially shaped object that is used to join two things together. Brackets are often L-shaped: each side of the L is screwed to one of the objects.

circular saw
saw with a blade that goes around in a circle, instead of backward and forward

crowbar
long, strong piece of metal that is used to lever things apart or lift them up

effort
in a lever, the effort is the force that goes into the lever to start it moving

force
something that either moves an object or changes the direction or speed of its movement

fulcrum
in a lever, the fulcrum is the part that the lever turns or hinges around. The fulcrum usually stays still while the other parts of the lever move.

load
in a lever, the load is the part that the lever lifts or moves

materials
in a building job, the materials are the things that the building will be made of

simple machine
something that affects force (by changing its direction, or making it greater or smaller). Simple machines include levers, wedges, screws, inclined planes, pulleys, and wheel-and-axles.

spiral
unbroken curve around a cylinder, for example the ridge that runs around the outside of a screw. Spirals usually start narrow and then get wider.

Books to read

Making With Machines by Anna Claybourne (Wayland, 2020)

If you ever thought it would be fun to build a model of Archimedes' battle catapult, for example, this is the place to come. The co-title *Making With Forces* (Anna Claybourne, 2020) is also full of good ideas for fun, science-based activities.

Wheels and Axles at Work by Maggie S. Wesley (Enslow Publishing, 2022)

Discover more ways that wheels and axles are used every day and how these simple machines are used to make more complex machines. While some examples may be familiar, others may surprise you.

Screws Keep Things Secure by Andi Diehn,
illustrations by Micah Rauch (Nomad Press, 2023)

This book explores the different kinds of screws and the many ways that we use them every day. You can ever learn how to make your own Archimedes screw!

Places to visit

Exploratorium
Pier 15, San Francisco, CA, 94111

The museum has displays showing many different kinds of science in action! Try making your own simple machines and learn more about how machines work.

The Strong National Museum of Play
One Manhattan Square, Rochester, New York, 14607

This is a fantastic museum aimed completely at young visitors. You can do your own experiments, play educational games, and learn more about different kinds of science.

Answers

From page 13

Wedges and levers both change the direction of a force. Wedges push the force outward, but levers usually reverse it. This means:

Axes = wedge

Doorstops = wedge

Seesaws = lever

Oars = lever

Nail = wedge

Scissors = wedge

Wheelbarrow = lever

From page 17

1) The screws turned the turning force into a pulling force, which pulled the screw into the wood.

2) If the turning force was reversed, it would become a pushing force. The screw would be pushed out of the wood.

From page 21

Pulleys affect a force by changing its direction.

The more pulleys you have, the less effort is needed. But as the amount of effort gets less, the length of the effort gets more.

From page 23

Rory's hammer (when he uses it to hammer in nails) is a Class 3 lever. This is because the effort is in between the load (the force being applied to the nail) and the fulcrum (which is Rory's elbow). In Class 2 levers, the load is between the fulcrum and the effort. In Class 1 levers, the fulcrum is between the load and the effort.

From page 29

The wheelbarrow is a lever, and has a wheel and axle.

The axe is a wedge.

Mo's scissors are levers. They also use a wedge shape to cut the packet.

The sharpened sticks are wedges.